Dedication:

To Diggory.

May your seeking heart
Always find what is
True, noble, right, pure,
Lovely & admirable…
And along the way,
May you discover that persistence
Is the key to the best kind of adventures.

Love, Mama

Oh no! Diggory has lost his lion.

Where, oh where can it be?

“Will you help me find it, Mama?”

asked Diggory.

“I have looked EVERYWHERE.”

“Of course!” said Mama.

“Did you look under the chair?” asked Mama.

“Oh, I forgot about there,” said Diggory.

He scrambled off to look under the chair.

What do YOU see under the chair?

“My truck!” said Diggory.

“Thank you, Mama!

I have found my truck.

But I still haven’t found my lion.

Will you help me?

I looked EVERYWHERE.”

“Hmmm,” said Mama.

“Did you look under your bean bag?”

“Oh!” said Diggory.

“I didn’t think to look there.”

Diggory ran to the bean bag.

What do YOU see under the bean bag?

“My rattle!” said Diggory.

“Thank you, Mama!
I found my truck
and my rattle,
but I still haven’t found my lion.
I will NEVER find my lion
and I looked EVERYWHERE!”

"Well, Diggory," said Mama,
"Have you checked under the couch?"
"Oh, yes! I will look under the couch,"
said Diggory.
And off he went to search under the couch.
What do YOU see under the couch?
"My hammer!" said Diggory.

"Thank you, Mama!
Now I have found my truck,
my rattle,
and my hammer,
but I still haven't found my lion.
Will I EVER find my lion?
I looked EVERYWHERE!"

“Did everywhere include the shoe rack?”
asked Mama.
“Oh, no, it didn’t,” said Diggory.
“I will look in the shoes!”
And away Diggory ran to the shoes.
What do YOU see in the shoes?
“My dinosaur!” said Diggory.

“Thank you, Mama!
Now I have found my truck,
my rattle,
my hammer,
and my dinosaur,
but I still haven’t found my lion…
and I looked EVERYWHERE!”

BEFUNKY PLUS

"I wonder if you looked under the stairs,"

said Mama.

"Oh, yes! The stairs!" said Diggory.

And off he ran to look under the stairs.

What do YOU see under the stairs?

"My lizard!" said Diggory.

“Thank you, Mama!

Now I have found my truck,

my rattle,

my hammer,

my dinosaur,

and my lizard,

but I still haven’t found my lion.

And guess what?

I looked EVERYWHERE!”

“Did you check the little end table?”

asked Mama.

“Oh, I don’t think so!”

And away Diggory ran to the end table.

What do YOU see there?

“My lion!” said Diggory.

“I looked EVERYWHERE and I found my lion…

…and my truck,

my rattle,

my hammer,

my dinosaur,

and my lizard!

Thank you, Mama!”

www.ingramcontent.com/pod-product-compliance
Lightning Source LLC
LaVergne TN
LVHW021321160826
845679LV00001B/442

* 9 7 9 8 8 4 6 4 4 9 1 0 7 *